This Coloring Book belongs to:

_____

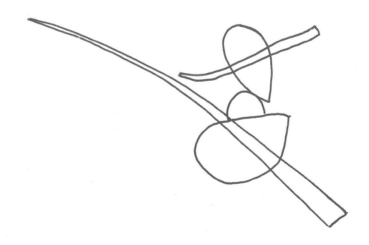

Coloring Book

Wassily Kandinsky

PRESTEL

Munich · Berlin · London · New York

That's Wassily Kandinsky, the painter.

He was born a hundred and forty years ago in Moscow. He studied art in Munich, Germany. Later he moved to France. He lived there in a suburb of Paris until the end of his life, aged seventy.

As a young man, Wassily Kandinsky belonged to a group of artists called Expressionists. They wanted to express feelings, dreams, and ideas through their pictures. To do so, they used colors that were not necessarily natural. For example, they sometimes painted horses completely blue, faces green, or cows yellow!

As time went on, all "real" objects disappeared from Wassily's pictures. Mountains, houses, riders, and trees all turned into patches of bright color. In other words, his pictures became abstract. If you look closely and use your imagination, you can probably make out animals, eyes, trees, instruments, and many other things.

In this book you will find pictures by Wassily Kandinsky to color in and finish yourself. Use your favorite colors. Paint the pictures the way you want. What colors and shapes do you like best?

This portrait shows the painter aged 47, in front of one of his paintings.

This is a photograph of Wassily with his painting class.

Where are these two riding to?

Here you can paint a big landscape on both pages.

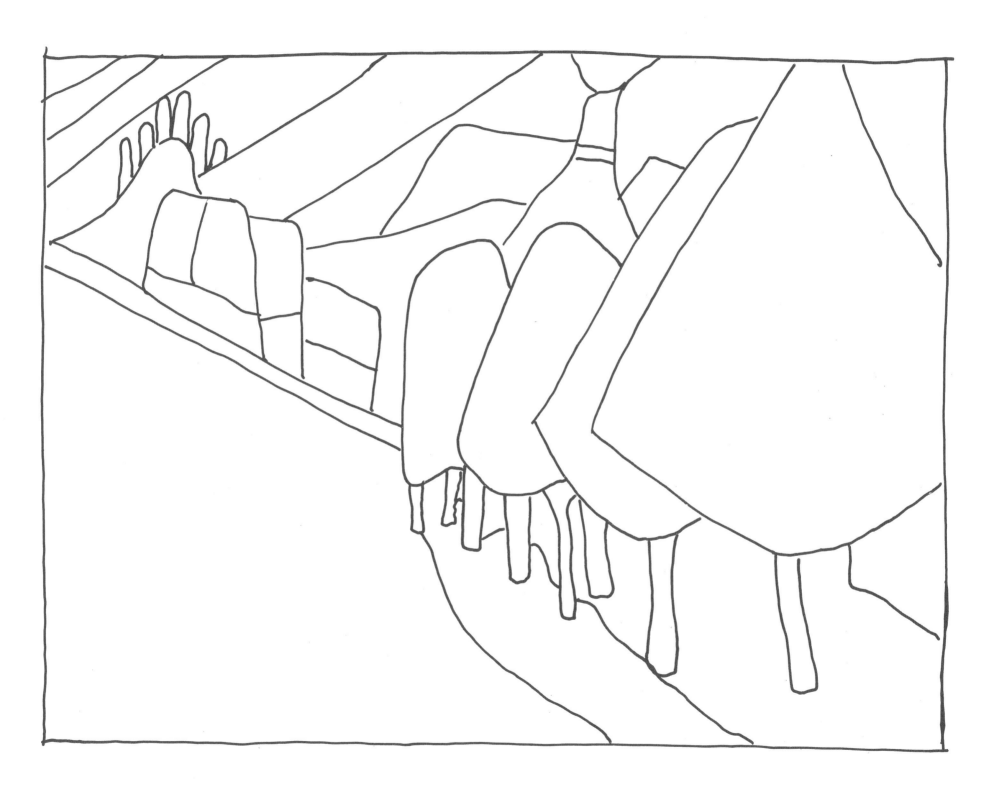

... and in fall colors.

Brighten up this picture with some lively colors.

How about painting some more men in turbans?

Can you help Wassily finish this picture?

What colors are these horses?

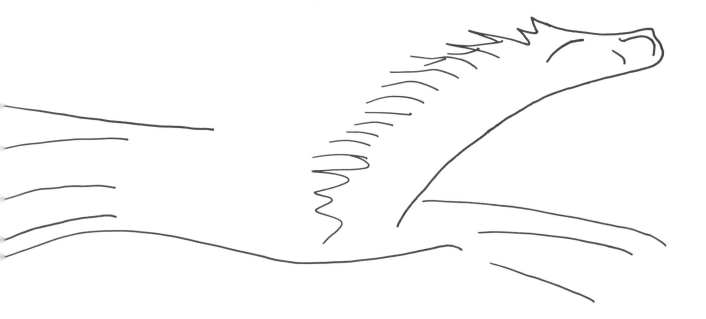

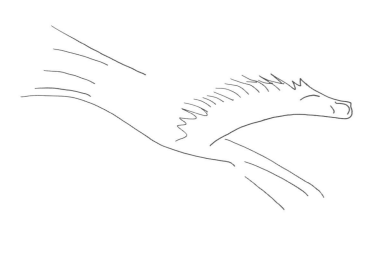

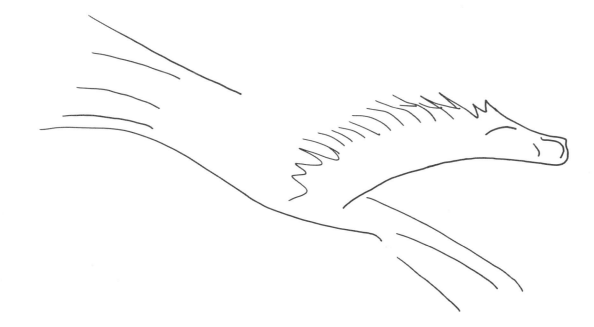

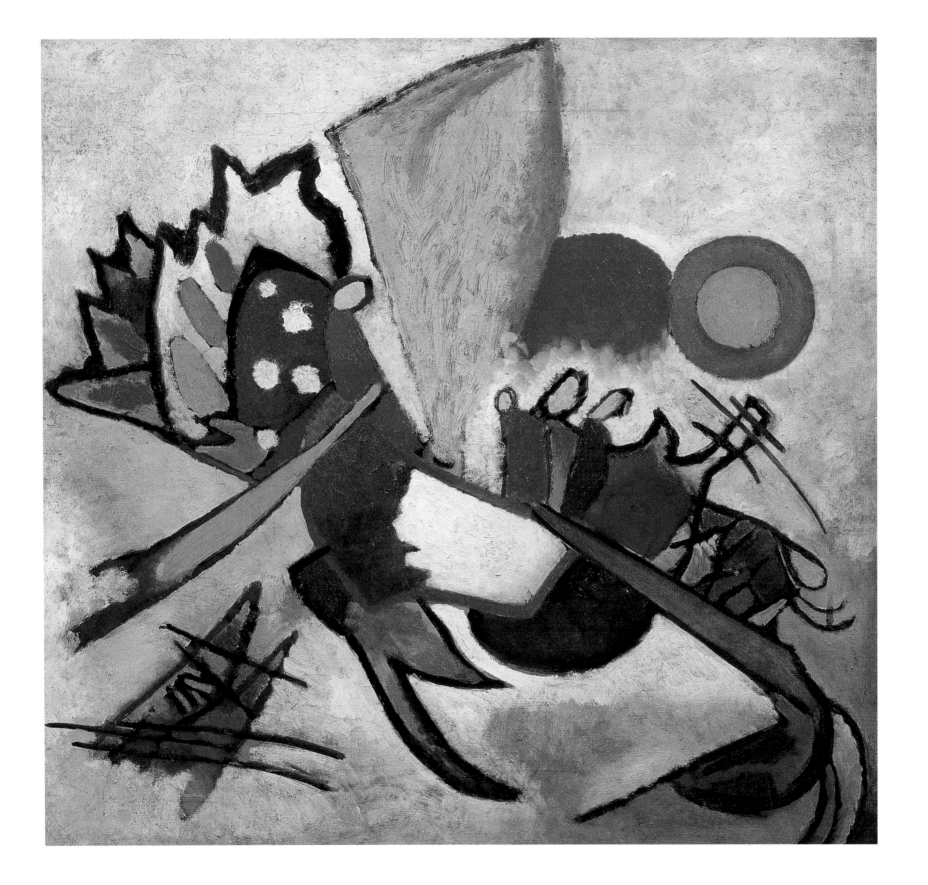

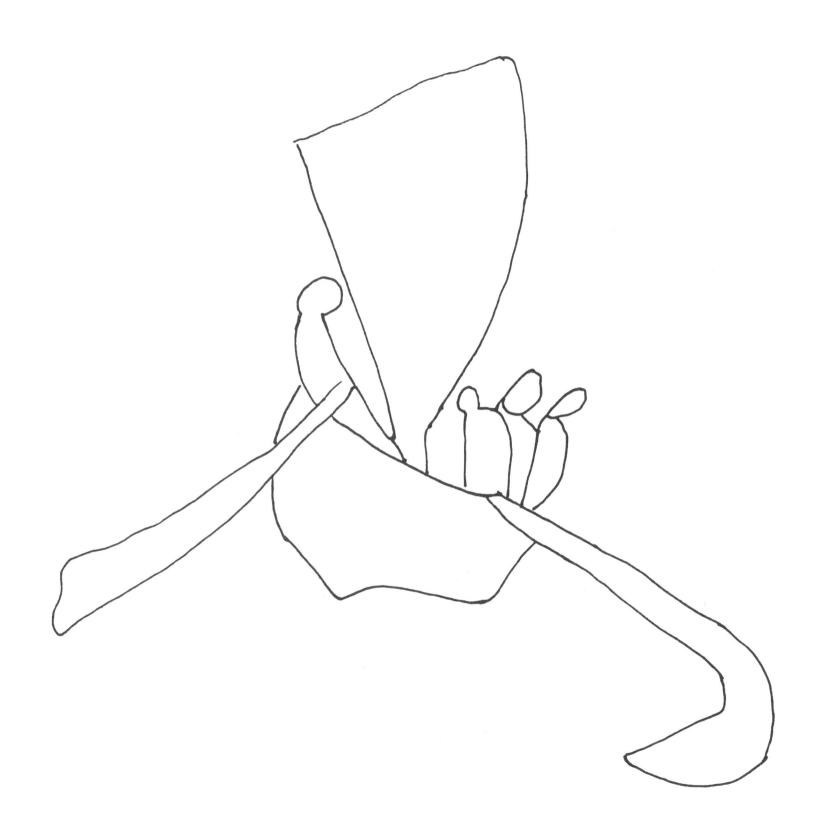

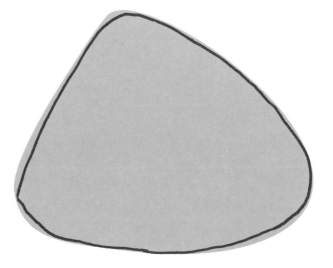

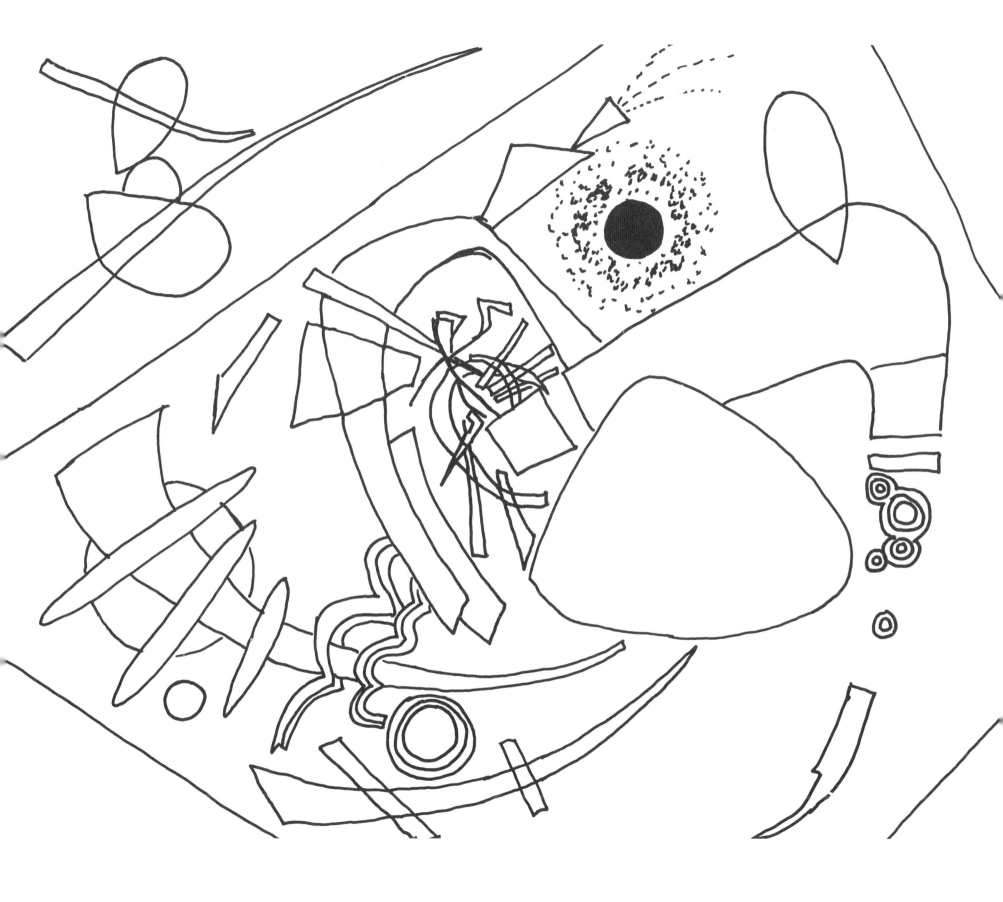

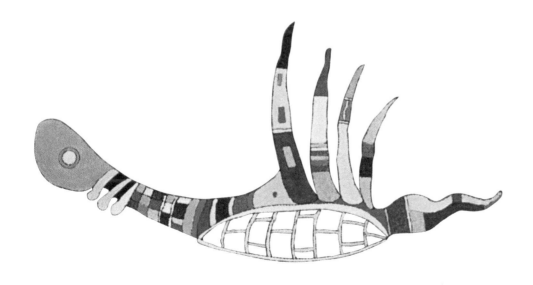

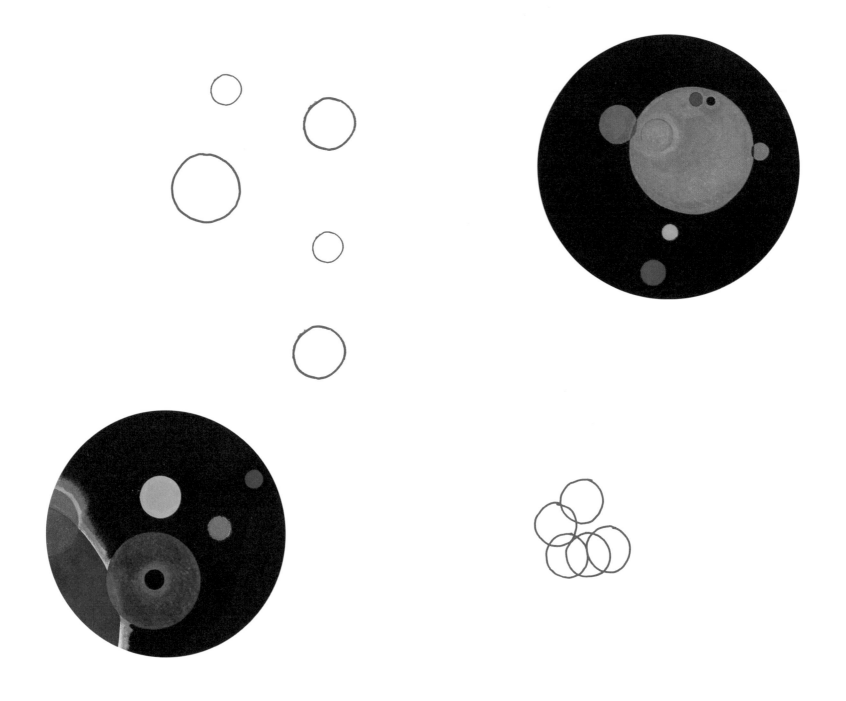

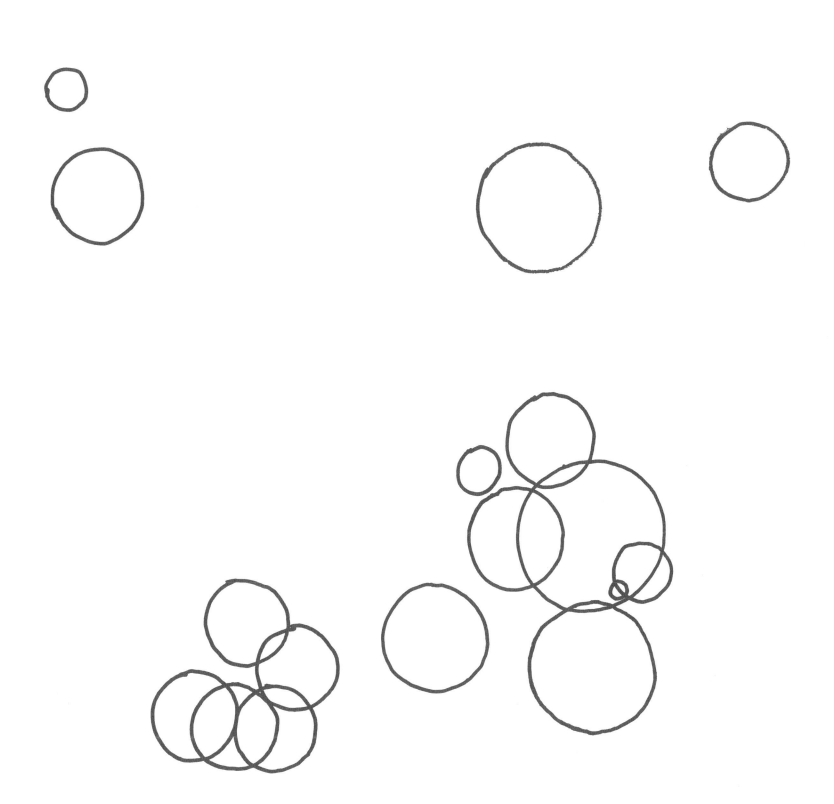

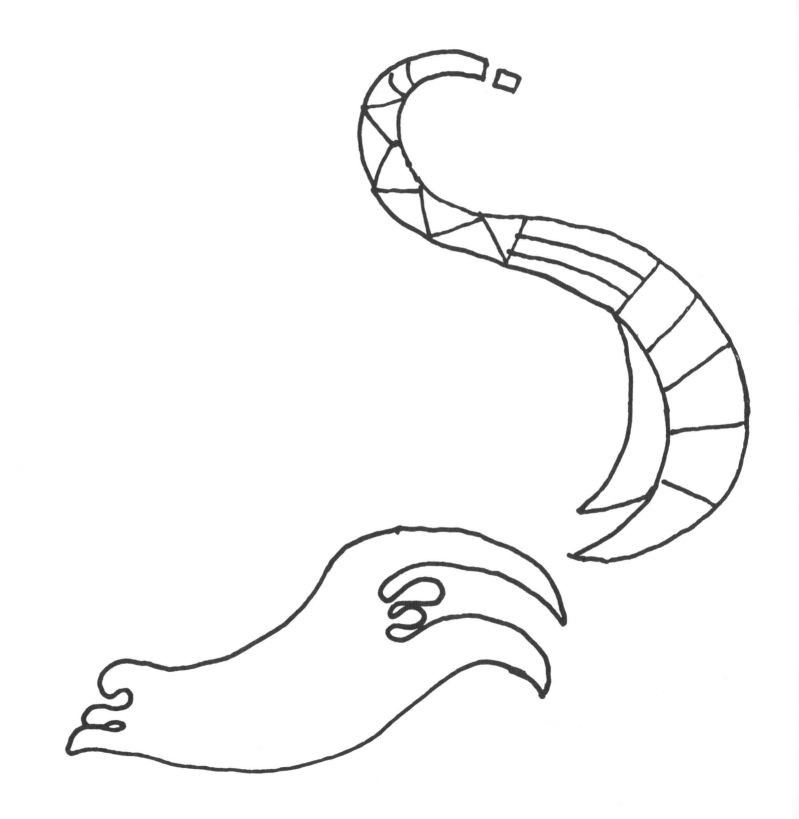

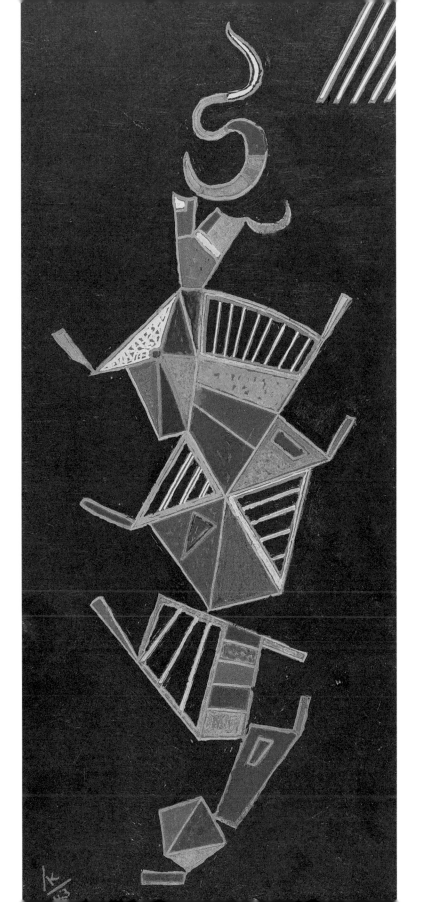

The Original Pictures by Wassily Kandinsky.

These are the pictures by Kandinsky that were used in this book. Which ones do you recognize?

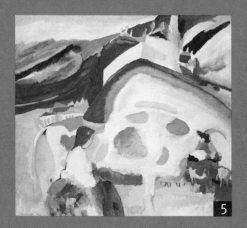

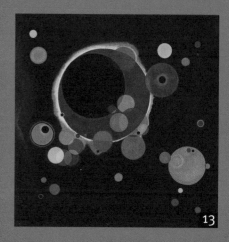

1 *Murnau—Castle and Church*, 1909. Städtische Galerie im Lenbachhaus, Munich. Photograph: Artothek

2 *The Blue Rider*, 1909. Musée National d'Art Moderne, Paris. Photograph: Artothek

3 *Sky Blue*, 1940. Musée National d'Art Moderne, Paris. Photograph: Artothek

4 *Improvisation No. 209*, 1917. Art Museum, Krasnoyarsk. Photograph: Artothek

5 *The Cow*, 1910. Städtische Galerie im Lenbachhaus, Munich. Photograph: Artothek

6 *With the Arrow*, 1943. Kunstmuseum, Basle. Photograph: Artothek

7 *Lyrical*, 1911. Museum Boymans van Beuningen, Rotterdam. Photograph: Artothek

8 *Oriental*, 1909. Städtische Galerie im Lenbachhaus, Munich. Photograph: Artothek

9 *Couple Riding*, 1907. Städtische Galerie im Lenbachhaus, Munich. Photograph: Artothek

10 *Red Spot*, 1921. Städtische Galerie im Lenbachhaus, Munich. Photograph: Artothek

11 *Improvisation 6 (African)*, 1909. Städtische Galerie im Lenbachhaus, Munich. Photograph: Artothek

12 *Nature study from Murnau I*, 1909. Städtische Galerie im Lenbachhaus, Munich

13 *Circles*, 1926. Solomon R. Guggenheim Museum, New York

ndon · New York 2006

80539 Munich
17 09-0
) 38 17 09-35

el Publishing Ltd.
, Bloomsbury Place, London WC1A 2QA
Tel. +44 (020) 7323-5004
Fax +44 (020) 7636-8004

Prestel Publishing
900 Broadway, Suite 603
New York, N.Y. 10003
Tel. +1 (212) 995-2720
Fax +1 (212) 995-2733
www.prestel.com

Library of Congress Control Number is available

British Library Cataloguing-in-Publication Data
A catalogue record for this book is available from the
British Library.

The Deutsche Bibliothek holds a record of this publica-
tion in the Deutsche Nationalbibliografie; detailed
bibliographical data can be found under:
http://dnb.ddb.de

Prestel books are available worldwide. Please contact
your nearest bookseller or one of the above addresses
for information concerning your local distributor.

Translated from the German by Paul Aston

Concept and drawings by Doris Kutschbach
Text by Natalie Buchholz
Design and Production by Claudia Weyh, René Güttler
Origination by Reproline Genceller, Munich
Printed and bound by Aumüller, Regensburg

Printed in Germany on acid-free paper

ISBN 3-7913-3712-2
978-3-7913-3712-8